34272279R00025

PATTIE FITZGERALD
Certified Child Predator Safety Educator
Founder, Safely Ever After, Inc.

Pattie Fitzgerald is the founder of *Safely Ever After, Inc.* and is recognized as a leading expert in the field of childhood sexual abuse prevention education. She is certified as a Child Safety Educator and Child Visitation Monitor, and has been working in the field of child advocacy for over fifteen years. As a **former preschool teacher**, Pattie blends her expertise as an educator and, more importantly as a **MOM**, to teach parents and children everywhere the most effective, up-to-date safety strategies WITHOUT using fear tactics.

Admired for her positive approach, Pattie has created her unique brand of *"Safe-Smarts"*. She is a highly sought after guest lecturer and keynote speaker throughout the country, addressing the need for stronger child safety legislation and sexual abuse prevention education within our schools.

Her *Super Duper Safety Rules* and curriculum are used in school districts throughout the United States.

Pattie is also the author of *"NO Trespassing – This is MY Body!"*. She has been featured on Good Morning America, ABC World News Tonight, CNN Headline News, MSNBC, and CNBC. She currently resides in Santa Monica, California.

"Safely Ever After, Inc. was created because... I'm a MOM first, who simply wants my daughter to be safe and still have a childhood that is fun. Keeping our kids safe shouldn't mean being scared or worried all the time. It means being able to navigate through the myriad of statistics, research and information out there, and empowering ourselves with the best weapon around: PREVENTION EDUCATION!"

Pattie Fitzgerald

safely ever after, inc.

For more information, please visit **www.safelyeverafter.com**

REMEMBER:

The **ONE** thing that deters a child predator or a molester is the possibility they could get **caught!**

▼

If they think **YOU** are paying attention and alert to their tricks...

If they think your child is confident enough to recognize thumbs down behavior, or may speak up...

YOU significantly lower the risk of being their target!

To remove bookmark cut along dotted line.

SUPER DUPER SAFETY RULES

1 I am the BOSS OF MY BODY.

2 Watch out for... TRICKY PEOPLE.

3 Safe grown-ups don't ask kids for help... especially when you're BY YOURSELF.

4 ALWAYS ASK FIRST before you go anywhere or take anything... even from someone you know.

5 NEVER GO ANYWHERE or take something from a STRANGER... even if they seem nice.

6 My PRIVATE PARTS are PRIVATE.

7 NO SECRETS about "thumbs down touches".

8 If Lost: FREEZE & YELL or ASK A MOM WITH KIDS FOR HELP.

9 I will ALWAYS TELL my parents if I get an "UH-OH" feeling.

safely ever after, inc.

www.safelyeverafter.com

Resources and Links

The following resources provide information, education, and advocacy for the safety of children and the prevention of childhood sexual abuse.

www.safelyeverafter.com – Safely Ever After, Inc. – Prevention Education and Advocacy

www.missingkids.com – The National Center for Missing and Exploited Children 1-800-THE-LOST

www.parentsformeganslaw.com – Parents For Megan's Law Resource Center and
                                    The Crime Victims Center

www.klaaskids.org – Klaas Kids Foundation

www.nsopw.gov – U.S. Department of Justice, National Sex Offender Public Website

www.themotherco.com – "Ruby's Studio: The Safety Show" (children's video)

www.thesafeside.com – Founders: John Walsh and Julie Clark (safety DVD's)

www.darkness2light.org – Darkness To Light – child safety and sexual abuse prevention education

www.stopitnow.org – Stop It Now – child safety and sexual abuse prevention education

www.amberalert.gov – National Amber Alert System (U.S. Department of Justice)

www.childhelpusa.org – Childhelp USA – 24 hour crisis intervention, information, and referrals

National Child Abuse Hotline: 1-800-4-A-CHILD (1-800-422-4453)

Additional Recommended Reading

For Children:
> *NO Trespassing – This Is MY Body!*   by Pattie Fitzgerald
> *Some Secrets Should Never Be Kept* – by Jayneen Sanders and Craig Smith
> *The Berenstain Bears Learn About Strangers* – by Stan Berenstain and Jan Berenstain

For Adults:
> *Protecting the Gift: Keeping Children and Teenagers Safe* – by Gavin de Becker
> *Predators & Child Molesters – What Every Parent Needs to Know* – by Robin Sax

Preventing Abduction

While statistics indicate that most child abductions are familial in nature and not by a stranger, there are some important precautions. Do not rely on the outdated *"stranger-danger"* concept. Empower kids to recognize **"TRICKY PEOPLE"** and potentially unsafe situations.

For kids who are out and about:

- Always use the Buddy System… while walking to school, hanging out in the neighborhood, or waiting at the bus stop. Children who are alone are more vulnerable targets and more easily "tricked".

- Don't take shortcuts thru alleys or isolated areas. Stick to well-trafficked areas.

- Walking To School: Establish a "safe route with safe-stops" along the way where kids can quickly go if they get scared or feel unsafe (*a public store, business or trusted neighbor's home*).

- Don't put your child's name on the outside of their belongings. A child's *"stranger-danger radar"* is short-circuited when someone calls them by name.

- Kids should not walk with headphones on or while talking or texting on their phone. Stay alert and aware of your surroundings. Kids who appear distracted are more easily victimized.

- If followed by a car, run in the OPPOSITE direction. If followed by someone on foot, cross the street and get away from them as quickly as possible. Run AWAY from danger, never toward it.

- Instruct kids to never get into a car unless you've already given permission ahead of time. This goes for people they know and people they don't know.

- Consider giving your child an "Ultimate Safe Grown-Up List" of 2 or 3 people that they can always go with. For example: *"your best friend's mom or Auntie Susan"*.

- Check First – before changing plans or your route, before going into someone's home, or accepting a ride. If you can't check first, then the answer is *NO* – don't do it.

- Go "Bananas" – if they're ever grabbed, kids should drop their belongings and scream, yell, and call attention to themselves. Shout out: *"I need help!"*, or *"This is not my father/mother!"*.

- If someone says *"Don't yell/don't run"* – kids should do the OPPOSITE. Yell and run! That person is basically telling you that if you scream or run, they will have to STOP trying to victimize you.

- Safety is more important than being polite. Teach kids it's okay to say *NO* and get away quickly anytime they get an *"uh-oh" feeling* from someone or something. If you feel scared, confused, or worried: trust your instinct. It's better to be a little impolite than unsafe.

- For emergencies: use a family *"code-word"* for children over the age of 8. If someone else tries to pick them up by saying *"it's an emergency – your parents sent me"*, kids must ask the code-word. If that person doesn't know it, it's not safe. Say *NO* and get away quickly.

Red Flags / Warning Signs

Red Flags can often be early signs of a sex offender's grooming process. Please use common sense. One red flag does not immediately indicate that someone is an offender, but does suggest that this person's behavior be monitored more closely. More than one red flag should be taken seriously, and steps should immediately be taken to protect the children from possible abuse.

- Someone who continually tries to arrange "alone time" with one child, often with lots of reasons or excuses why this is necessary.

- Someone who repeatedly befriends one "outstanding/special child"; singling them out and lavishing them with an extraordinary amount of praise, attention, or gifts.

- Someone who uses guilt tactics when you insist on setting boundaries or limits to their relationship with your child.

- Someone who insists on being overly physical with a child (excessive hugging, tickling, wrestling, lap-sitting) especially when the child has asked them to stop.

- Someone who often uses "accidental touching" or "touching games" as a way of being physical.

- Someone who makes inappropriate comments about a child's looks or body.

- Someone who continually invites children to spend time alone at their home, enticing them with the latest video/computer games, gadgets, toys, etc. – especially an adult who does not have children of their own.

- Someone who repeatedly ignores social or emotional boundaries or limits.

- Someone who shares inappropriate personal or private information with a child, that should normally be shared with adults only.

- Someone who frequently points out sexual images or tells suggestive/sexual stories or jokes with children present.

- Someone who frequently enters a bathroom or locker room while children are changing or showering, and does not seem to respect a child's need for physical privacy.

- Someone who frequently offers to "help a parent out"; i.e. baby sitting for free, providing transportation for a child, taking a child on an outing or appointment that would normally be done by the parent.

- Someone who ingratiates themselves into a family's lifestyle and daily activities, with offers to relieve parents of their parental duties.

- Someone who prefers to spend most of their free time with children and seems to have no interest in relationships with individuals their own age.

- Someone who seems particularly preoccupied with one child.

- Someone who seems "just too good to be true".

14 Prevention Tips For Pro-Active Parents

1. Use the anatomically correct words for body parts. Teach kids to use this language.

2. Remind your child that its always OK to say "NO" to anyone whose actions make them feel weird, yucky, or uncomfortable… including an adult or a bigger kid.

3. Teach your child to use active phrases: *"Stop touching me"*, *"I don't like that"*, *"You shouldn't touch me like that"*, *"My privates are private"*.

4. Listen to your child. If they consistently don't want to be around a particular person or environment, don't force them. They may be sensing a "red flag" that you are unaware of.

5. Question if your child suddenly has gifts, toys, or expensive items that you didn't give them.

6. Let children decide for themselves how they want to express affection. Don't force kids to hug or kiss another person if they are visibly uncomfortable doing so.

7. Trust your instincts and let your child trust theirs. Our instinct is one of the best barometers for letting us know when something or someone is "thumbs down".

8. Empower your child by practicing personal safety strategies in an upbeat manner, without using heavy scare tactics.

9. Find teachable moments to review a rule… while driving to a playdate or other outing, while setting the table at dinnertime, etc. Role-play, using non-fearful "what if" scenarios to reinforce skills.

10. Be alert to any sudden sexual behavior or knowledge that your child exhibits which is not appropriate for their age, maturity or developmental level – especially if they have new words for their private parts. Look into reasons why and consider who may have shared this information with them.

11. Let your child know that it is never their fault if someone tries to trick them with an unsafe touch. Make sure your child knows that they won't be in trouble for telling you and that you'll always believe them.

12. Be a visible parent: Get to know others who interact with your child on a regular basis, i.e. coaches, counselors, teachers, parents of their playmates, etc. Put out that "vibe" that you are involved in your child's life – it can be a strong deterrent.

13. Start the safety dialog with your children early on by giving them information in small "tidbits", a little at a time. No need to overwhelm your child with boring lectures, scare tactics or complicated concepts.

14. Make it a practice to have your child share details about their day... while at school, a playdate, or during their after-school activities. Keep it light and conversational. For example: "Tell me three things that happened in your day and I'll tell you three things about my day". By sharing information about their day, your child may give you clues or information which signal that you need to intervene on their behalf. And, even if everything is going great, this is an excellent way to foster ongoing, good communication within your family.

What Parents Can Do...

Step 1: Know The Facts

- 90% of childhood sexual abuse happens to children by someone they know, not by a stranger.

- Even when it is a stranger, that person will most likely approach a child with a friendly face and an enticing trick or lure… which means your child's *"stranger-danger radar"* may not ever kick in.

- Don't expect obvious outward signs in a child molester or predator. These people work very hard at concealing their true nature. It is our job to be alert to the "clues and cues" in someone else's behavior, language, and intentions.

- Child predators don't look like "the boogeyman". They are usually outgoing, super-friendly, and helpful… sometimes to the point of being almost "too good to be true".

- Child predators use deliberate tricks and ploys to gain a child's (or a parent's) trust. It's called "grooming". It's very calculated and can go on for weeks or months as a way to test a child's vulnerability or a parent's naiveté.

- Once this is accomplished, they will then proceed to victimize their target.

- Grooming consists of a lot of flattery, attention, physical affection, special gift-giving, favors to parents, often progressing through various stages.

Step 2: Reduce The Odds

- Most childhood sexual abuse occurs in a secluded or private environment.

- Pay attention to anyone who continually insists on one-to-one access with your child which excludes you.

- Assess each situation/relationship individually… sports coach, music teacher, camp counselor, relative, family friend. (Not all "one-to-one" scenarios are dangerous.) Use common sense by paying attention to "red flags" to determine who should and should not be allowed to have **access or private time** with your child.

- Show up early or unannounced on occasion if your child is alone with an adult.

- Be aware of much older children who have few age-appropriate friendships and seem to prefer being with younger children most of the time.

- Pay attention to your child's mood after spending time with certain people or in particular environments. Do they seem withdrawn or uncomfortable? Can they clearly tell you how the time was spent or do they seem uneasy?

- Keep boundaries clear and specific for those who interact with your children. For example: a music teacher should not offer to babysit or provide lessons for free, a coach shouldn't take one special child on an outing "overnight".

- Check several references on baby sitters, camps, nannies, and others who care for children, no matter how they come recommended. If anything seems "off" or "odd", listen to your instinct and do not put your child in a risky situation.

Parent's Guide

safely ever after, inc.

www.safelyeverafter.com

Check out our **Parent's Guide** on the following pages...

Remember BOSSES:

You are very SPECIAL and very IMPORTANT.

Now that you know your Super Duper Safety Rules,
you can be a safe, smart **BOSS OF YOUR BODY**, just like me.

- The End -

Rule #9 – I will always tell my parents if I get an "UH-OH" FEELING!

Bosses, **YOUR FEELINGS** are very important.

If someone or something makes you feel scared or unsafe, we call that the "UH-OH" FEELING.

It's like a little warning bell inside you that tells you when something just doesn't seem right.

Pay attention to your warning bell.

Remember Bosses: If you ever get an "UH-OH" FEELING, even from someone you know, tell your parents or another safe adult right away so they can help keep you safe.

Rule #8 – If I ever get lost, I can FREEZE & YELL or ask a MOM WITH KIDS for help.

It's important not to go wandering off when you're out with your parents, but sometimes kids can get lost or separated from Mom and Dad when there's lots to do and see.

If you can't find your parents, "FREEZE & YELL". Just stay right where you are and call out in a loud **BOSS** voice. **Chances are they're still close by and will hear you.**

OR...

You could ask another **MOM WITH KIDS** for help

OR...

the **CASH REGISTER PERSON.** They have a microphone and can make a special announcement for you.

BOSS REMINDER:
Your parents would never leave or go back to the car without you — so **NEVER** go outside to the parking lot to look for them.

Stay where you are!

Secret or Surprise?

A surprise is *different* than a secret.

- A surprise might be something like a party that you're going to or a gift for someone.

- A surprise usually makes you feel HAPPY inside, not scared.

Rule #7 – No Secrets...
about thumbs down touches!

No one should tell a kid to keep a secret from their parents... especially a secret about your body. If any secret makes you feel sad, confused or just plain yucky, tell a safe grown-up like your MOM or DAD, or maybe another grown-up you can trust.

If someone says **"Don't Tell"**
You should always TELL!

Smart **BOSSES** don't keep secrets, especially secrets about touches.

What about Safe Touches?

A doctor may have to check your private parts to make sure you're healthy. That's okay, **IF** your MOM or DAD is with you at the **doctor's office**.

And sometimes when you're little, your parents might help you stay clean like when you take a bath. That's okay, too.

But **no one else** should try to touch your private parts for any other reasons.

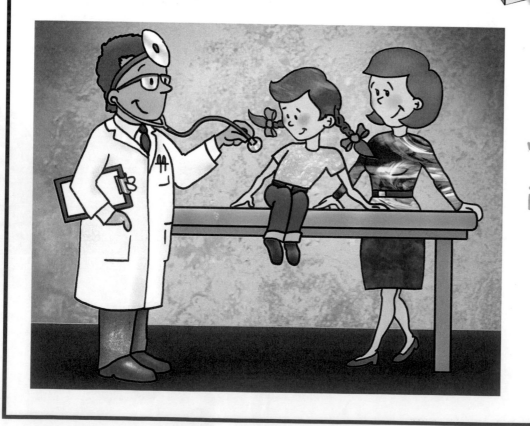

"My body is **MINE!**"

Rule #6 – My PRIVATE PARTS are PRIVATE!

Everyone has special parts of their body that are covered by a bathing suit. Some people call 'em private parts.

The Boss Rule is Simple: Our "private parts are private". That just means that no one should try to play a "touching game" with the private parts on your body, and no one should ask you to touch the private parts on their body.

We call that a "thumbs down touch", 'cuz it might make you feel yucky or scared or confused.

 You can say **"STOP TOUCHING ME!"** to **anyone**, even a bigger kid or a grown-up. Then go tell a safe adult right away... like your parents, a grandparent or even your teacher or school nurse.

Thumbs down touches are **NEVER** your fault. It's always okay to tell.

Rule #5 – I won't go anywhere or take anything from someone I don't know... No Matter What They Say!

Smart bosses never go anywhere with someone they **DON'T KNOW**... even if they *seem* nice.

- **Not** for candy

- **Not** for money

- **Not** for toys

- **Not** for nothin'!

If you don't know that person,

don't go with them – no matter what they say!

Take a giant step back and *get away fast*.

Rule #4 – ASK FIRST... and get permission from your parents before you go anywhere or take something even if it's from someone you know a little bit.

A smart boss knows you should never go into someone's house or car, or take a treat from someone unless you already have permission first.

If your neighbor invites you into their home to play a video game,

ASK FIRST!

If the ice cream man invites you into his truck,

ASK FIRST!

If a friendly grown-up at the park asks you for help or offers you a special toy or treat,

ASK FIRST!

If you can't ask first, the answer is **NO**!

Rule #3 – Safe Grown-Ups Don't Ask Kids for HELP... especially when you're by yourself.

It's okay for kids to help mom and dad with chores around the house, but other grown-ups should **NEVER** ask kids they don't know for any kind of help.

If someone wants you to come closer to their car to help them, say **NO**.

If someone asks you to help them find their lost puppy, say **NO**.

It's a TRICK!
Get away fast
from that tricky person!

Remember: Safe grown-ups ask **OTHER GROWN-UPS** when they need help... **not kids!**

What do tricky people look like?
That's a good question.

You can't tell who's tricky just by looking at their **FACE**. A tricky person might wear nice clothes or even smile. It's not what they **LOOK** like, it's what they **SAY** or want you to **DO**.

That's how you'll know!

If ANYONE wants you to break your safety rules, it's a trick!

Get away fast
and go tell a safe grown-up, like your Mom or Dad, right away.

Rule #2 – Safe Bosses watch out for... TRICKY PEOPLE!

Most people want kids to stay safe. But some people might try to trick kids into doing things that are **unsafe**. We call 'em **TRICKY PEOPLE**, 'cuz they try to break our safety rules.

Being a **SMART BOSS** means you won't get tricked!

Rule #1 - I Am The BOSS OF MY BODY!

Did you know that you are so **SPECIAL** and so **IMPORTANT**...
and that you are a **BOSS**, too?

That's Right! Even though you are a kid,
YOU ARE THE BOSS OF YOUR BODY!

Being the boss of your body means you're
in charge of any kind of touch that involves
your body.

If someone tries to touch you in any way
that makes you feel

SAD

SCARED

Or Just Plain YUCKY

You can say STOP

...even to a grown-up or a bigger kid.

It's **YOUR** body and...
You're the BOSS!

What does **UnSafe** Mean?

UnSafe means doing things that might hurt us **OR** make us feel **YUCKY** or scared.

UnSafe means we are **NOT** protected.

It's a **BIG THUMBS DOWN!**

Getting close to a stranger's car when you're by yourself is really **UnSafe!** That's a **BIG THUMBS DOWN!**

Let's take a look at some Super Duper Safety Rules so you can be a smart **BOSS**, too!

What does **SAFE** mean?

Being safe means doing things that won't HURT us.
Being safe means we are protected.
Being safe is a big THUMBS UP!

- Wearing a helmet when you ride your bike is thumbs-up safe.

- Looking both ways before you cross the street is thumbs-up safe.

- Staying close to your mom or dad when you go out is thumbs-up safe.

Greetings From
Super Duper Safety School!

I'm Sammy, the BIG BOSS here at Super Duper Safety.

My job is to teach kids how to

STAY SAFE!

Dear Parents And Caretakers,

Would your child know what to do if…

> • They got lost in a store or a public place?
> • A "friendly" stranger asked them for help?
> • A baby sitter or family friend wanted to play a "secret touching game" & told them "not to tell"?

Teaching our children about personal safety doesn't have to be scary. The purpose of **Super Duper Safety Rules** is to give kids the fundamental safety "do's & don'ts" that make sense and leave them feeling empowered without being fearful.

Consider this: Most kids understand the concept of rules. Whether they're at home or at school, on the playground or participating in a game or a sport, children know there are certain acceptable behaviors and guidelines (rules!) that everyone is expected to follow. Believe it or not, kids actually like having rules… because rules establish a clear-cut system and give structure as they navigate through their world. It's how they get through their day!

The **Super Duper Safety Rules** simply let children know what is "thumbs up and thumbs down" in the world around them. In the simplest terms: when kids are clear on "the rules", they are more likely to take action or tell us when *someone else is breaking a rule*!

Whether it's to keep them safe around someone they "know, don't know, or know a little bit", the **Super Duper Safety Rules** are an effective way to start the dialog so that kids will be less vulnerable to the tricks and manipulations of a predator.

It's not necessary to read the entire book to your kids in one sitting. Try working on only one or two rules at a time to keep things simple and build on their safety education.

Lastly, we don't want to raise children who are fearful of everything. Please approach the safety discussion with your child in a relaxed and nurturing manner. Keep it light, make it fun! Empower your children and give them confidence.

Safely Ever After's mission is to educate families with straightforward, common-sense information that actually works!

Warmly,

Pattie Fitzgerald

Pattie Fitzgerald
Founder, Safely Ever After, Inc.

*Please see our **Parent's Guide** at the end of this book.

Super Duper Safety School

By Pattie Fitzgerald

For Mark and Marissa... the reason for everything
and
For Parents and Kids Everywhere... that we all live "safely ever after"

Special Thanks:

Danna Teal
Linda Perry
Barbara Gervase
Jack Bills
Jennie Pica
Vin Pica

Text Copyright ©2013 by Pattie Fitzgerald   Illustrations Copyright ©2013 by Paul Johnson
ISBN # 978-0-9847472-1-4

Published by Safely Ever After Media

safely ever after, inc.

For information regarding permission, contact:
Safely Ever After, Inc.
1112 Montana Avenue, #277
Santa Monica, CA 90403

www.safelyeverafter.com

Printed in the U.S.A.

Super Duper Safety School

By Pattie Fitzgerald

safely ever after, inc.